Praise for *Crazy Louise (or La Conversazione Sacra)*

Crazy Louise (or La Conversazione Sacra) weaves both sides of reality's sacred and profane everyday cloth for us. Louise spins her daily life into a resilient bibliomantic poetry that's alternately and simultaneously condensed, diaristic, epiphanic and notational in its centeredness. "The grandeur / was refreshing" and always lands like a cat on its feet in the details: a "pink rose on her shoes / / Fragile / means..." When I try to describe Louise Landes Levi I use epithets like "unanthologized Beat," "our itinerant holy woman," "crazy wisdom deva", "divine translator of Sanskrit and French: Mirabai, Daumal, Michaux..." She is a poet of most holy email scrolls from & to the beyond. Here lies Poetry with a capital P's contradictions and contra-traditions of love and abuse, language in real life, in real time. Read these ragas of the infinite where "The Music is A Map." Let LLL into your poetic family tree Mandala: You are transformed. In Louise's own words:

"THE TRUE SUBJECT OF POETRY IS THE
LOSS OF THE BELOVED"
    And "The TRUE PS / Wasn't / it Rimbaud who
said when the female poets come, we won't even
recognize them. / this was before pop stardom,
/ of course // CRAZY is an attempt to touch
the untouchable & to release the power of the
untouchable

—LEE ANN BROWN

I'm thinking it may be helpful for you or the reader to have articulated in prose at the outset—or not=--but at least to have written—for yourself—what you describe to me, the break down of boundaries regarding sexual chakra. A statement, just to write out the story. Its prominence.

Where does the narrative belong? Or maybe that first poem is set off from the others as a preface in itself?

From what you say I think you should leave it as is. Yes the book heals! For what else are we here and writing poetry?

—LAYNIE BROWNE, from a letter

T0155238

Follow Crazy Louise, weaver of light body from trauma's dross. Herein lies the language of sacred madness, the language of truth, the great resistance, the poet's tongue is armored with the power of the Word. See Crazy Louise walk the high wire, swoop loon-like below the subconscious, Oh Acrobat of impossible gesture! Alchemy available. See Crazy Louise untwist, untangle, unmangle, the warp, the weft, the woof, pained memory is woven through.

This is what I said to you on the street . And what i didnit say but what I meant... LLL is one of the last of that poet tribe: The ecstatics, who carry the map of where the universal meets the personal. Those poets who make manifest the world are losing sight of, as surely as we are losing the glaciers, the world of connoisseurship, of scholarship, of magic, the world of heroic lineage.

—PENNY ARCADE

Crazy Louise

Crazy Louise
or
La Conversazione Sacra

Louise Landes Levi

Station Hill
of Barrytown

Published by Station Hill Press of Barrytown, Inc., 120 Station Hill Road, Barrytown, NY 12507, as a project of the Institute for Publishing Arts, Inc., in Barrytown, New York, a not-for-profit, tax-exempt organization [501(c)(3)], supported in part by grants from the New York State Council on the Arts.

Online catalogue: www.stationhill.org
e-mail: publishers@stationhill.org

 This publication is supported in part by grants from the New York State Council on the Arts, a state agency.

Cover design: Susan Quasha
Interior design: Sam Truitt

Cover photo: Ira Cohen
Rear photo: Louise Landes Levi (Giovanni Bellini's "La Conversazione Sacra," Chiesa San Zaccaria, Venice, Italy)

The publisher and writer would like to thank the following publications and their editors where some of these poems first appeared: *Wild Flowers*, ed. Shiv Mirabito; New York City Dzog Chen Newsletter, ed. Ed Goldberg; *Celestial Graffiti*, ed. Ira Cohen; *Big Bridge* ed. Michael Rothenburg; and *Banana Baby, Super Nova*, bi-lingual edition translated by A. Tuoni.

Library of Congress Cataloging-in-Publication Data

Landes-Levi, Louise.
[Poems. Selections]
Crazy Louise or La conversazione sacra / Louise Landes Levi.
   pages ; cm
ISBN 978-1-58177-145-9
I. Title.
PR6062.A494A6 2015
821'.914--dc23

CONTENTS

The Extreme Wisdom of Louise Landes Levi

This is a book for women, because they will find themselves reflected and projected here beyond what they have ever imagine or suspected about themselves, but it is also one in which men will find a visionary power and courage in facing exposure in the fiercest experience that is rarely recognized in women. Even the Tibetan masters usually ignored women's capacity for wisdom, especially for the "crazy" kind that informs Louise Landes Levi's book, and women as poets have been expected to limit themselves to "feminine" domains of sense and sentimentality.

Many female sacred figures make their presence felt in the book, starting with the Madonna of the Sacra Conversazione (the subtitle), who is listened to from her throne by a gathering of reverend characters. Machig Labdron, the Tibetan regent of a dimension of extreme, even disgusting and appalling experience, hovesr over many of the poems. The references to the mother and to women's love and suffering reflect, though they are not named, the aspects of the dakinis, their joyful, peaceful and wrathful manifestations.

But this is not a treatise on female spirituality, and what is more impressive here is the interpenetration (at times perhaps confusion) of levels of experience and awareness. The book opens with a disturbing encounter of the poet with the sexuality of her sick. indeed dying, mother, who is demanding satisfaction from her. Other poems about mother reveal her cruelty to the little girl, her "body beaten and broken", while late ones reveal forgiveness and compassion toward her. The nature woman's acceptance of apparent incoherence and extreme exposure must have been the necessary condition for forgiving—and in this way *Crazy Louise* tells us the process of becoming a holy madwoman.

"Mother" is the main theme of the poem. The ambivalent and ambiguous relation between the personal mother and the spiritual Mothers, wrathful, joyful and loving, is the tone of the whole. Love, abuse, death, sex are all suffused with it. Love remains under the shadow of rejection: "Mother flesh you do deny me." Ultimately, beyond this cauldron of sensations and insights, the mother is "the divine Mother inside," the source of psychic and spiritual growth. The muse, poetry, language is conceived as feminine, and this is related also to the spontaneous origin of the poems. So that in the all the threads of the book's complex world lead to the divine female source, which can be seem as both their origin and their goal.

Rowena Hill
Mérida, Venezuela, March 2011

Crazy Louise,
or
La Conversazione Sacra

A breakdown is a break through for a poet
L. Welch

Your contribution limits the population of Cats & Dogs
Highway 1

*

The government pays farmers not to grow crops
why don't they pay writers not to write
LLL

UNNECESSARILY

mystery
of love meeting, of salivas, of
panic, or trauma, or liberation

at the foot
of Mt. Labro & the master's

words & unconscious

(unnecessarily)

vibration

*

EARTHQUAKE IN BAGNORE:

followed
by: metro bombings
in
London/

The
world
is
surely at its end/ Benedict is
the last, or is he the second to last?/

2012/ the FLUORIDE

is

making us

CRAZY, O crazy Louise

what's to be done ?

*

Once
again, I am
Undutiful Daughter
as I refuse to kiss my mother's
pussy when her nurse fails to arrive—
Nurse is having baby — *Anyone can do that* she says — *you just have to fuck*

(Mother at her best this morning)

Last night she asked
if NN was my boyfriend
& finally admits Jacques is a "bad man"
I'm glad he's dead

Will D. find me unfaithful if I have.
a first & most probably last fling w. my mother/ I'm glad her
sexual energy is so strong—but am not sure if this mad passion
I want to eat you she
says
is coming fr. her mind or her body.

She helplessly commits acts she warned & threatened me abt:

**Do Not Walk Barefoot in The Hall * Don't Use That Kind of
Language**

&

cries

out

Fuck me Jacques, Fuck me

Is my mother turning me on
because this is the first time we've communicated?

When I look at you I want to vomit
—her consoling words at father's funeral
but now I'm her darling daughter

Adorable.

In those days broken bones & bruised—even burned—
face
&
body
meant nothing to the "officials."

We are good Jewish children fr. good Jewish families:

I'm

sorry

Jacques fucked you when you were 2 or 3
or 4 or put his finger where one wld.
put
instead
a
penis
you generously instruct.

*

JAI MA

O Virgin of Guadalupe,
Sophia—O Mother

As usual,
I'm a bad girl—unable
with my poet's tongue to definitely make you come,

to satisfy you when for years I've been singing to
the mother—Jai Ma
I can't satisfy
this
last
request

———

I finally understand
your mother's boyfriend satisfied you both,
for years *Men like pretty little girls*
you
say—

then *it's not always nice to be so pretty.*
*

I don't want her here. I don't want her,
You cry to my father
When he invites me
to
visit
It's yr. home
he
says

helplessly

*

The only thing I can think of to do
w. my grandmother's $ my paternal grandmother's
is: start a press:

If you have a book you'd like me to look at, please

Send it to:
Mother

ORAL SEX,
box 69,
Taos, NM

***

If you sleep w. other woman or not,
Why can't I share my sisters? Is this a sacred act
or not, is it less sacred
or more, if shared.?

Mother
is arousing me
w. her enfant like confusion/ whose very touch
was terror—body beat & broken.

Is this the ultimate healing
I've been waiting my whole life for?.
or is that death? As Allen said.

*

Will my life long conflicts
dissolve in yr. cunt, dear Mother?
or must I go to

KALI

I'll get Hanuman
to do the proof reading
proof of his Mercy & Immutability
coming to my Rescue
keep what is for me
& of me,
near

It's hard to say No to Mother
I love to suck dick but my mother's pussy ?

Am I being UNREASONABLE,
a BAD child
once
again.?

*

W. Palm Beach & NYC 2001

Hanuman to the Rescue, a well known comic in the Indian genre.

Did
the Master appear
or was it I who appeared
ragged
&
in
need
nourishment?
Did
the moon rise
over the pacific, just
for us, you thought it was a head-light/timing too
precise, O too precise, yr. kindness,
– in dimensions we do not know-

Unable

to

realize

even in this one,

O you who relate to the Kingdom of Ants

Please keep us
in
Mind.

———

AL- ZAWAHIRI

THERE WAS $25,000,000 ON HIS HEAD
THEN SOME FREAKED OUT AMERICAN SHOT HIM DEAD

I find it inconsiderate
The $
shld. have gone to
start an orphanage in Kandahar
or toward the purification of the water system in Heart,
No doubt bombed to shit.

Not only do the rich Americans fuck everything up—
They don't even bother to distribute
the $25,000,000

OFFERED

for Al- Zawahiri's head.

———————

"1 homicide per minute
on
Planet
Earth"

Kids
are getting cut up
& left in bags in the bottom
of valleys
or
lakes
They
are left on street corners
on
165th
& Broadway

O Really it's a bad time
for
Planet
Earth

———

POST MODERN

BAGNORE
takes its "commerce"
<u>seriously</u>

Sans $

even

on

Sunday

————————

Nirvana is Samsara

la bycyclette fa anche male

ha detto

Viola.

*

The
MISTAKE
I made this winter
was
trying to work in Anna's just because
it was a good place (to work)
in the summer.

*

My Dear City Cats, Sept.30, Bagnore, Gr.

I hope you are well & looking after Marlene.
What do you think of her new friend?—I do hope yr.
not jealous—for jealousy is a terrible obstacle. But guess what?
A cat's squatting in the tower!
I don't even know its name— or obviously—
its gender. The squatter scared me at first but now
I've said to him or her 'don't worry stay for the winter if you like'
One less homeless cat—Right?

Hope to see you both soon,
love
L.

Manny & Topolino

c/o M. H. Hennessy
508 e. 5th street. No. 10
NYC NY
10009
USA

Aphorism

Don't take a job you don't want

_____

Don't

want a job
you
can't

do

*

Message
fr.
cemetery/ignites, my
sad heart/ here flowers, weep, bend, unite,

all I cld. not do for you,
all I cld. not do.

Passionately, you sought. One single
stone. One pearl.

In
whose doe-eyed
gaze, Sensational Ass/ We took the human birth &
raised it

A
new
octave

whose Nature

far

surpassed:

Opacity & Oblivion/...... Apocalyptic light shielded us/
fr.
(illicit)
congress,
as
you drew in—one breath—then the other,

Ever
watchful, you,

open
my
treasure chest
of
attributes
&
eucalyptus,

& bathe, in the
stranger glory of
the

night,

Come, quickly.

*

R.K.Dick/even in
Bagnore, feeling the bliss
of Machig Labdron,

I am
centuries
young,
&
never
victimized,

by childhood rapists, by
mothers burden, by any male authority,

I reborn, resist
this war between, the
greater balances, of nature,
of human
nature,

I am THAT I am,
reappropriated, it refers to my CUNT, it refers to
my Warmth, my Desire, to Love

you.

*

Sudden

      space, the mt. brings me into the fields/

                  again,

      Snow, walking in mt.,. D. in distance, how to wake

      fr.

      COMA, OM A, OM...

A

*

      Sleep, dream, a man w/o a body/ Anna's again,

      practice at Merigar, White A & Chod. Is there such a
difference between Chod on Central Park South & in Gompa? Never

      dream,

      of

      NN,

      World is changing, everything going to shit, to war or is it
not changing & my lyricism, what I lost in Paris, what I found in
Rajesthan. I must work —finish CD & work harder,

      but must not lose craziness,

      It's a virtue

      after all.

*

Rereading
Bharatya Natya Shastra:
Primordial battle field/war has been, always
Because, because part of world/
SAMSARA/

Snow. Over weeping trees,
outside door, where did they go,
to make yr. house hotter
& yr. heart
cold,

Whispering, the trees, bring illness—
Cancer formation, black snake underground—
eat your skin—your energetic,
well-being

Louise write: to enter, subtle light, body.

*

DUNES

Nina
shows up/ w. the news
that (according
to
NN)

there have been
reports
that **SADAM HUSSEIN**
is
in
Margarita.

(*He was, after all, a friend of Chavez,* says the
Master)

Work w. the circumstances
he
further
says

We can use the money

Moreover/
transform Wrathful Deity
into secret bliss & clarity/ he has
come
to
us

to practice. Where US creates Demonic Apparition/
can we create Saintly

Ones? It's not a bad
"idea"?

(gradually, relaxing in Bagnore)

*

Sadam's sister practices
Namkhai Arte
on the beach
of
Saragoza.

The "Dunes" has a special entourage
worthy of their
"state of art"
security
system/

Sadam & family mingle w. disciples
over caviar/chicken & tight security watch/

A

*

It's
good to know
compassion still
exists in Vicenza of
all
places/

Were Rinzo Angelica & Dara
for
real?
am I/ I
discovered Mira in
a train station in Bombay
&
now
selling ('my') Mira—at train station—
I
buy
ticket
to
Bologna

*

Where
Krishna a-
waits, without
knowing I'm on my way
to
see
him

Krishna is/& isn't

_____

&
you are/ & you are not. The
wonderful fountain, the
sad
fact
is:

I really don't know
what to do with my Life.

Milano-Bologna 1992

*

POSTCARD to D.   9 Sept. 2007

Buon Giorno

I like the birds & wind & the NO taxi but Bagnore =
boring/the tower is sterile. Reports of Mobile Bacterial Weaponry
(USA)—of Immunity For Soldiers (USA)—Iraq is n Chaos/ No
Contact—No contact w. Merigar—No dance either/
Working a lot & doing

'BROOM OF INTESTINES'

is heavy & deep / try it—Practicing
at midnight is very nice/ OK,

I need a far out "home'"

90%
of my most neurotic
problem is the isolation I felt "at home"/—torture.
I need to see divine Mother
inside
Louise.

So call me/Kali Ma
&
relax.

w. LOVE, Kali MA

For Zion's sake I shall not be silent
until her vindication shines forth like the dawn...
No longer shall you be called "forsaken"'
and your lands "desolate"
but you shall be called "beloved"'
and your lands "espoused."

*

Do not grieve. I will deliver
you fr. all sin & evil.

I will seek your nothingness to invite you
to myself. for all you give me
I give you my heart

I want you to be All mine

*

Now

That/ UNDONE

I

am

OFFERING

*

In
the crystalline
whirlwind, 30 birds &
I took refuge. One had yr.

NAME,

I
was a tree, then a current
of
transparent white, transparent
pink,
golden:
I
perceived.

the
car was yr. father's. The Moon
was

mine.

Purple,
      I

            behold,
  Red.
     The letters were written

  & some
    were
      read.

     Later

           the currency of the
                    country
                      made

          exchange/ impossible

             *

I
stayed
beneath the Sandalwood
&
sang.

*

You, passing thru/
invisible walls,
enter
my
heart

flower, heaR

*

Moonlight

I send Rays

of

love,
of essence

of internal
light, of secret

light

*

SE
        a ti, se a ti
     Si a ti/ per casa

piace

          LA POESIA

     stai zitta/ da partutto—from
     the sofa, the chairs, the chandelier

     STAI ZITTA. Shut the FUCK UP

             UP

             YOURS

 Se

   a ti, piace, piace, piace, si a ti piace: Let's
     Fuck. Do you like me, like.

          LA POESIA.

The

      Body of, Extinction
      the
        stars,

     Pleiades, The belt of,

                ORION

That star is important for practitioners/

        Lately,

                  fading

       ladies & gentleman

    that star is important for practitioners

          *

On

the star of,

DAVID: We're dancing

On it,/ every evening,—a flower

consumes/

as the 3rd & 4th & 5th & 6th

EYE/ An eye for an eye,...

I bow, at the
foot, of the luminous,
Master. I master the series
of delicate   OVER TONES/

UNDER TONES/
due to the threat, of ignorance
& pride, I found you—the sun
setting, the sun rising

the PLURALITY

Junk is No Good
& you lay down prayer.

& the birds wings were

ruffled/

*

"Ladies & Gentlemen"

A Chi? a Ti piace
per
casa

LA POESIA?

Now:
study the names of

Stars
&
places/ the planets, the "issue"

in Bagnore was the Privatization
of the Hot Baths

*

REclaiming

the Permission, to LIVE

what happened when I was "small"—

for which to forgive, entire generations
of the victims of the massacre

in

BOTISANI

where
my head rolled

to ? / beneath the saddened eyes
of my 5 children—

I was only
23/ whose shock waves endure for
7 generations, as you drop me on my head & tell me

it was you who

should

cry.

*

I
awake this
morning/ my landlady announce that
a corpse wld. be hard for her to handle/ she's a real bitch,
felling the forest in front of the DOOR, her house—the largest
& in her pockets enough to sponsor the 10,000 poets—sitting here,

peacefully, amid

pines
&
shadows,

Shadow
of yr. father, on a train
in No. Italy, bound for Treblinka
bound for Baden—Baden, *Arbeit macht*
aber hij will nicht ___& takes die gelt
& hears the cries—he survives
& they do not survive &

you ask me not to lock the door,
as if my body
was
not
"mine"

*

After
the dark, I notice
I, I AM **THAT**—I AM—

I AM / SHRI YANTRA. it's only
the beginning. I notice the unbearable beauty
of the Red & Gold horizon, the colors,
are
overwhelming

but they do not

blind.

*

I wld. like
to speak (& thus to spread) the lavender ashes of yr. gaze or
frail perfume. Is it Love, Is It Love?

&

the privatization of the waters
in Bagnore was a dream & the Hotel Gaia
had not been bought by the Multi-Nationals, who wld.
close down the village & still proclaim

PEACE & LOVE

on the sign in the park
reserve for their clerks
fr.

Milano.

*

You
speak thru the
stars, the dimensions are
transparent / I DREAM: when I come here I am paralyzed,

but
now
I
can
walk,

a, lone
a,   LA/ LA

HO /Poetics./& the method

"was"

travel, She
wasn't
the first one to
swim
in

the
dark.

*

I want to be someone
Johnny Depp
cld.
like,

Seriously,
I don't have to meet him,
or anything,

but
since dreaming abt. him

a few weeks
ago

when seeing
him in Eva, here in Italy, EVA,
get it,

EVA,

I realize,
I really want to look like

someone, he wld.
like/ that's a hard call,

but not impossible/

I'm a slow developer/ but
the anima, must
not
be
repressed,

Gradually
I will transform,
fr. your favourite lady 'hobo,' into
someone
Johnny Depp
cld.

really
like

*

The
hunters in Santa Fiora
were satisfied w. *cinghiali*/ they were
organized to murder every little wild pig
that hid fr. them in the soft green bush,

It
didn't really matter,
you know, a Jew, a wild pig, the
point was to kill—
to kill en masse & to kill
as a group, a proud group.

Thank
goodness, those Australian
aborigines, recognized in the frail man's group,
for survivors of sexual violence, the
next line, in
the

dream/

They
chose those wounded men,
because the wounded men will heal
the killer instinct, that waits on the road

w.

a

rifle

even
the wild pig,
has brothers & sisters,
a mother, a father & a
home

somewhere.

*

COR /CAFe.

I can't wait until
there are 12 in the circle

Maybe, it's better to

BE/ just
holy—to transmit
that to suffering world/

It
wld. definitely be very nice
if you were here on Kloveniersburgwal to
watch the night fog on the Canal

to gaze out
fr. bright window
to
dark.

*

The quietude of
the Japanese
print,

The Wisteria
was
not/
noticed,

You give it back, *party party.* D.
cut yr. dreams/write like
Kerouac/
keep on writing.

I want to write the future

He's a Poet of the 22nd. century

WINSTON KINGDOM SALON

2004

*

It's strange how
my view is so (tantric)—I can't
dissolve it because I was saved by it...

Peacefully perfect/
CAFe, Illusion/ White cat (black)

cat/ Greek

*

"BEYOND" all this

the great

immeasurable

*

as usual I am
w. the undesirables/ *it's more fun—*

*

La Monte & ROSE,

Music,
now

SOFT.

*

F
  a
   l
    l
    i
    n
    g
down the Mt.

(My knee hurts)

falling in love

(My heart hurts)

Luckily. I'm not just surprised. A man's drunken

WORDS: He wld. like to be Hafiz

but

isn't.

O Louise. Why did you let

that

thief/

IN?

*

TUNISIA

PARTO VENDERDI

E. 102 RT ll AM-9AM

GENOA (Station Brigatte)

Sabato 2 pm—Domenica 11am Lunedi 8 pm Martedi 10 am

I meet Al Sayid at the train station in Genoa

(copy Arabic fr original)
*
a
lone bird
in
the
station

of
Genoa.

*

I

meet
Nagi Nasia
Presidente della Assocsazione Cous-
Tionide Democratica Comitato
Coordinemento

He watches my bags—he offers me a coffee.
&
to
visit,

via Bella No. 6 Furli 471—

tel. no. 33.9.62.88.452

*

The
        bird
& a prostitute
   fr. Africa
            are

            my
                    witnesses.

        It's
    cold in the station
    & I feel a great need
to change my Way of Life

            to
            BE,

somehow, / there w. you

                *

Nagi
gives me
his phone number. Says he'll pick me up at the
station
(in
Furli)

Mussolini's buried there
he
says.

_____

One learns a lot/ traveling.

***

CRIME

in

Italy

I'm
on the train,
to Venice. G. has
"stolen" w/o. asking, (of
course) my heart & I.
have symbolically

lost my crystal shaped
pendulum in the form of a heart. On the train I borrow
a pen fr. a serious looking musician:

The next thing I know is

Violinist forgets her violin/

I almost make her
pay for the fact that she did not GIVE me her silver\
pen which I had borrowed
(on
the
train)

tho she must have known I needed it,

but pursue her, crying
"signora signora, il tuo violino...."

In
tears she thanks me for her violin
& rewards me, at last, w. the silver pen.

The violinist was
Respectable—I was fascinated
by the musical notations
she was studying.

She
did not know I was a "poet". although seemingly disordered, I carefully
observed her & later, after she departed, her violin
abandoned,
in
the
train

*

I thought we'd stay here forever but we all went home—PW

NYC/after loss
Time & The Timeless

after losing my
computer:
I went downtown
to
Chambers & Broadway
Many many

computers
lost,
also husbands,
wives & eyeglasses
policemen
were also
unaccounted
for.

*

Airplanes
&
money
oil,

Beneath the Sea.

I want YOU
I want IT.

I need it
now
&
if you don't give it to me.
I'll tear yr. fucking balls off
&
totally
mess w. yr. mind.
I'll destroy it if I can.

Flags
fluttering
above So. Houston
& the Bowery.

222

Tibetan flags
&
when the AIR was
poisoned, the letters

"Baby you changed my life"

purified,
the mind & the body.

"NYC"

cld. not be put in a knapsack
& carried w. one

The Detchen Linpa said that.
I wonder what he meant.
That my travels
were over
or
that
the earthquake
which was "officially" reported
at 1:3O am

was

actually

a

bomb

beneath the island

"the bomb wld/ eventually sink Manhattan"

"Too many gay people"

& I wish you'd fuck

me in the ass at

11.:30 tonight

after meeting S & W

then

please

liquefy my cunt

& make me

come

&

tell me in that soft voice

"I don't like you"

&

mean "please fuck me so I don't have

to think abt.

my

mother".

After that
we went to the park.
We studied Hebrew Arabic Urdu & Persian
When Faiz Ahmed Faiz
read a poem

"The Loss of The Beloved is the True Subject"

50,000 people came to listen.

Mera zindage hazalemTera gum se achigahara
Tera gum ha dar ha kekut
Mera zindage se pyare

an important person
sitting in the front seat,

driving
across
town.

NYC 2001

We've
all been told

in
the

KALI YUGA

(respect)

for

(human)

life

will be

mineralized

still

it comes as

a

"surprise"

———

by surprise

shld. I quote
the
Master?

"When I look down (at my lotus feet I see… Nothing"

*

I want to

leave
the
City
"DYLANA NIRVANA"

Is
there anywhere where you
are
not?

The

    great

        sexual/

Rebellion/while, insidious fires burn

    "Samsara is always confusing"

      announced

        that

           OLD FRIEND

   of

     mine.

Does it matter if its more or

          less

              confusing?

Louise is crazy

She even lost her msc. "CRAZY LOUISE:

       *

Was

    I

a nurse

       or

just

    a

      "vagabond"

no one wanted me,
    but
      you,

how fortunate

*

Crazy,

they always said,
but it took you to show
me,

"Crazy Wisdom"

for NN, NYC 1995

The
day my father
DIED, DIED also
our

Love,

At
the grave
of my father
the TOMBSTONES /as
texts, reading them I/ wanted

to introduce you to my
ancestors, but
it was
too

late.

For NHL NYC Nov.2001

Afraid

to move, outside
the ZONE of the father
sadly,

why?

———

Afraid
of the unfamiliar,
deeply sensitive, like a deer in water,

he
died,

anyway

*

In the situation w. D., did I make things so terrible so
I'd have someone to "blame"

is there   anyone to
BLAME:?

in

the

uni verse

*

Is my mother to 'blame'? Do I try to
have someone to blame? (so I wasn't ready
or changed date of return.

Does
D.
arrange his power trip
&
need to reject, he

messed
up

Taos, almost
purposefully,
what
a
lila

*

& how Dakini like—R. Beer
seemed

powerful

(energetically)

but seemed to have some problems
w. 'women'/ I thought,
in retrospect)

*

Someone
shld. teach
the people who work
in
the

Alt.

not
to kill insects

———

That

particular face

I thought it belonged

to me—that's childish,

Nothing belongs to me

I am **Nothing**

yet

I am Everything

&

I love you.

but

you don't belong to me. Not even if

we make Ritual/ Love

in

Taos

&

the Universe is consumed/… I

really have

to

heal

Louise

———————

                    The
                 universe
             created these rules
                     &
     even

           if I don't like obeying,
             certainly, they can
             not be avoided.

                     *

             Thank goodness,
                     I
finally dreamed last might—at a festival for NORBU
Fabio & Cici were making love or doing something along those lines,
                 afterward,

                 Fabio

   sprayed clear water all over Her.

Was this transmuted spermatozoa
like the Urine, become gold,
of
Pemo
Tso?

There
was music for Norbu,
a composer I was to marry & didn't, at least
he asked me to sit down next to him, until his wife
arrived, & it was like I didn't exist, until I read
her obituary 20 yrs. into the future.

A lesson in impermanence
(but why was I so fixed
on sitting next to the
composer.
I
should have just
sat down

ALONE

*

You

played

the "real deal"
on the Piazza Navrona/Nirvana

*

The
grandeur/
was refreshing.

Why wake at all./don't wake,
Louise c/o Really Waking
&
forget abt. marriage,
find yr. place
on
Earth
&
invite yr. friends to share it. You're already
married. LORD Krishna
will definitely
not
abandon
you

———

Other
mothers dead
yes, but
never

my

mother.

Is
she alive
in the sky, in the sky of mind,
in the sky of my desire,
in my pain
at
her
departure,

She wasn't supposed to die,
other people's mothers
yes, but never,

"Betty"

"Betty, Betty"

where are you? Ben is looking for you,
down at Ratners, why aren't you coming in for blintzes & borsht,
your beautiful brother w. his long
wavy hair is waiting
for you to
come in to see him
but neither ONE of you exist anymore,

Sarah

wants to talk to you,
she wants you to forgive her,
she fucked all those guys,
trying to save the uncles I never met,
Frank & Dave & Abe &
also
Carel,

You wld. have had an affair w. him
you said, O so many things
you said
as
you took
your time dying & let the ghosts fly past you,
all around you,

O Louise I just saw Sarah you wld. say/ I understood. I
cldn't suck you off Mother, but I understood.
yr. asking me to
"play"
w.

you

*

I watched your elder body contort w. sexual desire,
but you were only 4 yrs. old,
something

was

wrong,

You don't have to call out for Jacques

He shldn't have done those things
to you—You're only 3 or 4—
&
you ripped up his picture
I'm glad he's dead
you
said
He'd been dead for years, but to you he was
alive, you OD'd on sexual pleasure sexual desire
before you were old enough
to

play

w.

marbles,

I
paid the price,
it cost me so much I
lay dying on the streets of Paris,
that great master Namkhai Norbu
saved me MAMA,

He'll save you too. Don't worry.
Your little box will go all the way to Deva Chen,
just
don't be afraid

You did a great job here (on earth)—you took care of orphan children,
if you were here you cld. take care of me too. Mama,
but don't worry.

I had a great time
on those piazzas & street corners,
I found a freedom so precious,
a love so immaculate, it erased any trace of imperfection.

Your sacred body citadel/ my unrequited love
paid off in the end,/ I *had* to find something
that didn't involve
the

other.

You
my first & only mother,
one day I will find you again,
& I will hear your voice, just like you heard
the voice of your mother, calling to you,

When I play my sarangi & hear all those
long long tones, I find you

I
hear your voice just like music
inside of me,

So don't worry, Mama,
I'm here. & I can

hear

you.

———————

Appropriately, the image,
descend, my lethargy, undone, nightmare, I
w. you, in the forest, in the tree,
trellis, the old roses, weep
for
the

Mother,

I embrace you, in sleep,
'I
love
you'

Withheld,
in those conversations,
fr. W. Palm Beach to San Raphael & Amsterdam. fr.
Paris, London & Bombay, to Great Neck, NY.

*

I thought you were my invention, I knew you cldn't be "for
Real", & then I learned/ the smell, the body, how
dear, the odor, the blue eyes, the cheek bone,

The last generation to sing
the Sh'ma
in
Botisani
has been laid to rest,
in Brooklyn, NY

How many billions of children
have put their parents in the deep dark of Earth,
yet it seems, I am the only one, mourning today, where
so long ago a quick fuck meant the end of retribution & you were
free to buy hats on 7th Avenue & to one day,
meet, Nathaniel.
You
were
free.
You
are still free, mother,
the deep, bend the arc, the curve of the coloring
light, that's you & I am here, transformed into deity, pray for you,
bind you to the eccentric light, ever ignited in the first kiss you gave me,
gone astray, the difficult passage never
binding, never too obscure,
the one gate,

gate gate parama gate parama gate

bodhi

svaha

Call
you home, light undeceiving,
no less an entity, my brave mother, my courageous sweetheart,
flown into whose abyss, finally, to perceive, the great joke, strangely, born
in my heart,

your red seed. your great seed,

MOTHER

*

Irrespective

of
WIND
&
the
accumulative

FIRE,
all along the horizon
visions, of
the
world

I sang, sung, was singing the
melodic line / my
birthright,
in the hours, grief, grieving,
what was the feast thought I to behold,

Longevity,
the neurons endure,

The flame is licked, licking, is tasting, your body, is

a

dream/

your mind,

the age of /predicament,
the sea, which takes you,/ further,

Pigeon, why did you leave me?

Saints, hover in the darkness, in the caves,
in the apparitional signature,
the higher powers,
attuned, tuned, tuning,

I intone, the death
the death giving light,
the messenger,
of
the
world

*

Before
I told her, later

always wanting/ punishment/
she had no way, to know/ now. rippling/on my skin,
what is left,
of
your
skin

sleepless, dreamless,
here are the signs.
I tried to

tell

my brother/ Let Her Be The easiest place
to be was where they wldn't SEE me, not to disturb, you tell me it is past,
but I am seeing, tasting, a (relative) garden, but a garden, now assailed,.

I'll be that spinster who goes to grave, flowers, flowering,
write your poems accomplish your work, gentle, undone,

A voice on the telephone,
a plea in a letter, to forgive, I forgive, I let flow, any vestige , of
repentance
mine.

it

It cld. be said more simply yet. I
Thee /

await

St. Marks, NYC 2001

The End of the Affair

If
his name
had been Schoenberg

&

not Schonberger/things
might have been / different,
at least

more

MUSICAL

———

Everything

to him/

was

Mother/

His store, his house, his "cunt"/ all
Mother, except "Mother"/ He
was astonishingly

OBEDIENT

————

He didn't like his Mother's
cunt when he was young—but
as he grew up he developed/

TASTE

*

The only trouble was he was afraid—
afraid to blow himself up, so he blew up
everyone else/ no wonder
he didn't have
any

friends,

at least, if his name has been
Schoenberg,
we might have

"played"

together

*

ADDRESS

Everyone
has trouble w.
my address/ does it exist
or NOT, actually this trouble is in their
minds, like all trouble.

Dorje Wangchok

NEVER
has "trouble" w. my address/ he knows
even tho' or because he doesn't know me, that
what I write on the envelop in the upper
left hand corner is going to be
where I'm at.

That's why I like those Rinpoche's,
they, almost
always,

KNOW WHERE ONE IS AT

*

Appropriate

the body, ritual—
morning, I arise, calm/ the voices,
the ANCESTRAL wing, now stilled/ we
are harmonic, first touch first, lithe.
musical, we are making,
love,
in
the

Equivalent.

*

I sing the body music /Sleep has cleansed
your mind/ it is the vessel of the

SPIRIT

the

MOTHER

Awakens,
all is quiet, I mourn, I grieve, I rejoice,
I
see,

You,
solitary,
but no more in pain, Mother, as dissolved,
the universe becomes who you are,
totally, I am, You, have been
always,

You.

*

VESELKAS

A
man w. a
nose like mine/ Sunday/

3. PM

———

Madonna's
brother's best friend/ Tuesday/

4. AM

*

A
drug dealer (fr. Hawaii)
religious devotee/ gone wrong/ A
Buddhist—he hands over $100.00 so I can hear
The Dalai Lama, who will teach The Gradual Path

Han Shen & Ling Repa, Thursday/

6. AM
*

all this/ at Veselkas

*

Don't Grieve—give to the world & follow
the Guru's instructions.

Black Book

(New Mexico/California - 2001)

It's
the year 2001—he
says

you ain't seen
NOTHIN
yet
as
I contemplate suicide
because my bags got lost
&
I cldn't spend
New Years
w.
D.

*

How
come you
always
show up—
just when

I'm abt. to

write

a
poem?

abt. you or
the

universe?

————

]   I'm going HOME/
              I don't want to go to
          where I came from/ Patti was
                    so
                         strong/
              She knew where
            she belonged & who
                she was
                 talking
                   to

                    She
                got all the
            TOP energies/ & I felt
        left out/
                 My brother
                  is

                   TORTURING
                      me

        I don't know if there's

                              $

                                in

                            the

                               family

If I was

        destined

    for

     STARDOM

I'd be Patti Smith. I'm

Louise

What exactly

  is

    POETIC

       INTEGRITY

Is the past UNREAL/

  or

    UNFAIR/.does

it

EXIST?

Did

the

forest

w. its ecstatic

wind

exist-

Did

I

honor it even

if

I

wasn't

Julia Butterfly

_____

Did
the sea exist/ or
the
desert?
When
David

looks out his windows
does he see
Me
TOO
or just
the dome
of
La Sanga de Christe

I cld. write

melodic
lines,
Now I can't
even

sing.

*

I can't

      sing.

I can't

       cry

_____

I have to be

   A

        Poet,

Again,

   not

   to

      think abt. it

but to $\mathrm{BE}/$ IT.

_____

I said it's unfair You said it's uncool
You always knew how I wanted to feel.

Lee Ann said
"write it now
invent/compose later"

Lorine Niedecker

STAR/fence/blade

Cid Corman

*

Mother Flesh
You do deny me

*

I
have to go to RAGA
room—*in the dream* (to find something) I
then drop NN's silver computer/ a
beautiful machine'-
in the dream
I feel bad to
drop
it.

(why do I go each day to computer
in "real" life
& not work on
4 contemplations?)

*

118

Many dreams
&
I am mostly awake in them.
I need / a relation—Organic/amazing practice.
I send energy to D., all chakras well except sexual one,
like cross wired or miss wired. maybe relation to P. wld. help him—
if he cld. have direct sexual contact w. someone.

Also took homeopathic remedy & it helped me—wish
I cld. give my mother Ecstasy—She is depressed.
They ought to have aphrodisiacs & drugs

FREE SEX
for
elders.

*my psychic reading of all this says
D. will not sleep
w. the girl

that "higher" forces
block this for reasons of inner work
related to his (or "our") "karma"?

*

JESUS LOVES YOU

GOD is love
GOD is All

had yr. greens today?

Can Vegetarians Eat Animal Crackers

In
a "forest"
of burnt-out
pines. The
palm trees
are
still
standing

*

Only the ladies can go over to the Rest Room,
You gentlemen can go behind a tree, if you like

(Highway One)/ USA

*

It's very painful to
leave the Sunshine State/
not just the sun,
leaving
the

sun
My
mother is living in a specialized mental
asylum, perfect
for
her
4 yr. old
mind,

She's
like a beautiful
doll
I'm going to kill you one day
she
says
Then
my strength is
only
fr.
you

She
is busy
free
associating

but
I did learn
that Samuel
worked
in
Gordon's Bath House

Jacques
was a furrier
married to Molly
& fucking both my mother
& her mother
or
something
along those lines

D.
AGAINST
my
"poetic"/—not
Totally—he also

inspired me
then I thought it
was
love

Mother was trying to understand
her life-long marriage
Where's poppy
she asks each day.

She said it was about
"fucking"
so
I tried to explain

the primordial ground

Yr. too intelligent for me she said,
Stop analyzing

Except
for my refusal to
sleep w. her I did
play dutiful
daughter
&
it got better & more sweet, too

Sitting w. her on the balcony
& dressing her
the last day

Suppose she rebels &
become a punk in the bardo
will
I feel defeated
No. Mother—KICK
                        ASS

Who sucked yr. pussy
where his penis shld. have
been? you remind me & where

at the orphanage, at your
mother's at your
foster-
parents

Don't despair
I pray you find my dad &
recognize that you
are

forgiven

The mad look
I saw on yr. face
when he had a stroke
& you threw me out, then drove
past the bus station
looking for me

7
birds
on the balcony
O mother, it is ALL/ sacred.

It is boring
you say—abt. the temple

They don't even want you at
the hairdresser
(your former refuge)

So
finally I show that
I'm not *that* mother, mother
&
always
loved
you.

my

Mother

W. Palm Beach-NYC 2000

126

How
come I'm
on a bus going to NYC
& NOT to
New
Mexico?

*

Radiant
SUNS have inspired
this
MAD
Verse

My mother's naked body doesn't
scare me
any
more

I'm dreamin' of You You You

Things are burnin' up so quick. I can't get warm

It's all about "nuts & bolts" birds & bees
it's abt. the play of opposites
I tell him.

*

We
cld write
a
novel,
uniting

Signs & Reflections
The man on the bus fr. No. India
was so fat I cldn't breathe
but
Faiz Ahmed Faiz
knew everything,
believe me, everything,

He was so drunk he forgot his wine
bottle at the mosque

THE TRUE SUBJECT OF POETRY
IS THE LOSS OF THE BELOVED

The
true medicine
for an unhappy
affair is conscious

Sex
in the style of
Guru Sahajayoginicinta

If you think this is a history
of the world, yr. right.
if you think
this justifies delaying my trip
to Arizona & Nebraska
you are wrong
&
have no right to call yourself'

Miss Amerika

W. Palm Beach-NYC 2000

I have
the feeling that
the heart shaped mirror lens
which I found in a purse in Florida
is
the one that
is missing fr. the
red & black rimed glasses
I left
in

NYC

*

Mysteriously

&

past

deadline,

my mind begins to work again.

Mi sento come uno bambino,

a pena

nata

(NN via email)

*

(transl: I feel like a baby, just born)

What great suggestive power
a little email can have when Namkhai Norbu
decides to contact lllevi32 @hotmail.com.

It's enough to place a cause
for
Enlightenment

O

Sweet Liberation where I study War No More

on
the
entire
INTERNET

*

Burnt out building
in
Harlem

—

'like a thief in an empty house'

Fragmentation & collage / KALI MA

one day Ill kill you

O MA MA ma
Wrong to "fuck" you –

He used to dress me, you report/ he did everything for me.

*

Rave
against
the child crimes of the century
of the civilization
of the mind

*

On

the train

to

Irvington

collage & fragmentation

*

Like

David

I refuse solutions fr. the past.

*

On the way to David.

I feel sort of

WEIRD– travel time

ca. 17 hrs. to Denver 19 hrs.

to Taos, I

wanted to fast—now feel sick,

frankly

I don't like doing the same thing, twice.

*

Valentines Day

OMAHA Nebraska
LIGHT
ENERGY
says the sign to
my left/to my right
GREYHOUND

A

blue VAN passes/ the lights are RED & become green. Does
this mean I shld. remember the state?
&
practice
Guru Drakpur & Green TARA

but there are
obstacles
strong obstacles
as
I sit
in OMAHA

& remember
OM OM OM A A

A

ha ha ha

OM

A

HA

Daughter of the Dakini

ON VALENTINES
DAY

*

O
David
REMEMBER
The sign in Lama
"Remember"

or

just relax
in this New Tibetan year
& hope I am the
first person D.
sleeps
w.

tho'
I was not the first one
of the millennium/ HO
Laughter of Dakini on Valentine's Day
He doesn't fuck her—*it's true*

too many thoughts of you

I
end up in Redhook
refusing Joel's
requests
or
advances
as
they
are
called
Did
I want to be
w. him/ was it
revenge/
or
pollution.

I
honored
my samaya & traveled
on
to
Taos.

Dear Louise

If you had honored yr. vow
to the Muse or gotten

K. to get yr.
ticket 7 days
in
advance,

you wld. now be in a
much
better
situation
already w. D. & having read at Penny Lane

Remember

MUSE

IS YR. KEEPER. WILL get you to places on time,

keep you well

NYC-OMAHA-TAOS 2000

*

Florida

is the State that did it

The suffering of Samsara is infinite even for the Floridians
They didn't protect their Blacks

******

'Bush knew the White House wld. be attacked, he was paying for it'

'Al Quada has been on the CIA pay roll for years.'

All this Florida Sun

but

A

in the Alt. on Avenue A in NYC
people are still saying thing
like
that.

*

TURQUOISE BOOK

The
Iranian, the Chinese
& 2 Black ladies fr. the Bronx
were 2 blocks fr.
DELANCEY STREET
&
didn't know it.

*

The
UFO was
reasonably luminous
for a Spring night,

No clouds/ Behind the clouds,
O Sun

O light

*

San Anselmo
2000

Arcadia
is disappearing / the

carefully constructed verses/ DC

is not subject to the effect
(of the Kalpa) it is intrinsically—
beyond
time.

*

Note: DC: Dzog chen, "the direct path—highest of the 9 vehicles of the dharma"

The
extraterrestrials
warn of an explosion
but
its only in the Enquirer
not in the NY Times.

Neo Fascism
is the mudra—itself
of the times/

except for the skin head
who fucks me in the Ass
in
Bologna

Remember
that I too was
raised in the temple
or not far
fr.
it

Meanwhile

my beau has once again proven
his total inability to be One.
Is that News or just the
Blues

as
I long for liberation & at times, I am
happy to report,

receive

it

*

Perched
over or beyond
Pacific/blue, water (?) :
It is not a ? of =/ of

equivalents.

I/AM at ocean
end, Franco, in the sea, in
the
stream

in the BARDO

of/
Repose

*

If

   he

      had

         not/ O great, Wheel

I TURN, my turn, turning, I give back, the wind,

          I breathe, Inward,

Upward,

         the head, home, MASS

of

   light. Masses/ He, humble, RECEIVES,

    (better

        than)

            the shrink. *A Bodhisattva*
            e sempre humile/ is
              always: humble
           It never takes birth or dies/

      JIVA ATMA/ *para atma/* his face
           suddenly
               stone. *It's a holiday,*

"The Music is A Map"

         *

Beyond doubt/

I
Attach, myself/ to the shape

of, the Penis-head & this flower's

mystery.

If I withdraw my energy
you will die O Mysterious

Mother.

*

O Ancestors,
Be in my embrace,

We
don't know
who's us & who's here &
who are you, awake in my dream

I dream of whose Vaster Continent,
in my bed, in my bed
of
dreams.

*

Notes
fr. (oral teachings of)
DUGU CHOEGYAL RIMPOCHE

purity, equanimity & bliss—
natural State of Presence/
relaxing ourselves in Natural /Mind.
self confidence, all 5 vehicles—in great equanimity of DC
beyond clouds—Sun. No point of this view in doubt
OM MANI PADME HUNG SHRI

GHOSTS: PRIDE, COMPETITION & COMPARISON

8 fold path

SHANTIDEVA

PARAMITA: INTERDEPENDENCE & SHUNYATA

*

MASTER
may look like human being but is actually something else.

The Nature of the Mind
is emptiness beyond rational thought.

Whatever objectifying thoughts arise
they proceed to the expanse of the sky of
sheer lucency.& at the end
are held in the kingdom
of the

UNBORN

*

Fr. whence,
my *fame* cometh/ comely the evening, the
rapacious priests/ The
Querelle hath
hurt/
my heart / Roses/
Roses/ Rosebud
was
her
name/
*
Buddha/ha ha ho
on the Bowery

an American genius/
the first one to exhibit in the LOUVRE/

in NYC
a phosphorescent Rabbit//
"Hello Amerika"
———

Ka Ka
it is the ignorance
& arrogance & attachment/
causin' all the problems/here, as elsewhere,
The modulated /
Up
Road,

I'm dreamin' green bucks, baby.

*

I'm
dreaming long ocean
& the Power. He took me
in his arms & didn't like it.
You believe in Love,

'Do not forsake me, O My Darlin'

*

The
ornament of expression/*Buddha
Nature is pervasive*, he said, I saw it in the
shining leaf, the ray of sunlight you wanted to
leave & I wanted
to stay/ A
typical
dilemmA
A
A

*

We
cld. spend a night in Phoenicia., our
old
flame
rekindled, my new

relation did not exactly
work

out

*

PILAR
was haunting me, me too, me first,
I wanted to say. So did Subadra, then they found
                                        her
                                            dead.

        The authorities had removed
                                the
                                baby

        We don't like junkies they
        said as if anyone thought they did

                    *

Beyond, thought,
great compassion, **Hail Mary**, My father .Who art, art thou whom
'I sought, the deadened bodies of the 21st.century. the millennium.
She said drying her eyes at City Lights Bookstore

'our people can be awful'

Angular & lean,
the old poet was anything but, my country tis of thee,
We landed here, the trucks on the Road,

going

North.

I want to be alone. I told him
& raise the FIRE & BURN/ that Night & I unite,
the solstice, be in my heart,

I am the Lord thy God.

I AM that AM I

Insight Glass, Inc.
Benecia Ca.
707.746.65.71
*

WWW.suckmydick.com
www.comeonme.com

*

154

D. & I
are arguing abt.
the benefits or non-benefits
(merits & demerits)
of using the mantra

OM TARE TU TARE TURE SVAHA

on a "commercial" record.
RELAX
I tell him
.

Knock, Knock, Who's there?
A A WHO?

A AH HA SHA SA MA.

*

A AH... The 6 syllables of the Vajra

Will
D. & I
make love
on
Valentine's

Day?
Will
D & I
ever:
make love
again?

While the entire world is at War
& the Monarch Butterflies are dying in Mexico, this is all I can think about?

*

CIA COUP D'ETAT
NEVER AGAIN

(on JKF Jr.'s shrine, NYC, 1999)

*

We

look for

the Road,

to

the

Ocean of Mercy

*

The village going

crazy. The young boys

crying Dalai Dalai

&

the thin white

scarf

s

u

d

d

e

n

l

y

*

"I am the name of the sound & the sound of the name.
I am the sign of the letter & the designation of the division"

The Nag Hamnadi

The 8 Rasas

sringara: erotic

hasya: comic

karuna: compassion

raudra: fierce

vira: heroic

bynakara: fearful

bihatsa: disgust

adbuta: amazed

santi:
peaceful

*

NIJIKA

In

      her

         black
            hair

                yellow buttons

On

      her

         black shoes

               Roses.

*

I'm
a living Collection
Staggering, zig zaging
Sixty trillion Cells, all Drunk

"Without images, soul lacks wonder, w/o wonder, no joy, no joy,
no magic no magic,
no glory.

Nobody told the flowers to come up,
no one will ask them to leave
when Spring is gone

P. Whalen

I
see an old acquaintance last night,
a poet I wld. sometimes meet, Merry Fortune.
she looks stronger & tells me how her mother, a few months ago,
mentioned to her that her father was not really her father but instead was
a Native American, long gone—this, casually, on the way to a train station,

along w. an 8-page letter,
abt. herself, not even abt. the long gone Indian
My friend who now looks like a Native American told me
she had had many dreams which wld. indicate such heritage & found
herself, in dream, at Iroquois assembly where the model for what was later
US constitution was drawn up

.She has now met some of her Indian brothers & sisters—
& is going to a pow wow in Nebraska—she always had such a clear view
of community & felt so alienated by poetry scene, even tho she worked for
St. Marks

for a while

*

Fragile

means, I can't stand the subways—I can't eat wheat,

or milk products—I have to always refuse when I want to accept,

it creates bad mental habits too,

that is

I have to refuse what I want to eat in favor of what is possible to digest.

When I go astray for 1 day there are no evil consequences

but when I go astray for more than 1 day which is likely

1 for I love the forbidden foods,

I get very sick.

Yesterday was an example,

then I remember my childhood & how I must have felt,

very often sick in that way

Recipe for survival:

No wheat. No lactose. On island, can get away w. indulgent

habits, more easily for the exercise & winds supplies needed O2 (

oxygen)—which is also obtained through digestion, usually, but not in my

case,

helas.

David
cashed in & became the recipient of a library
which Gary Indiana was giving away last night, by surprise.
I do not get along w. his friend JLB

but so much good fortune has come to him via JLB—
someone who works for him also works for Gary
& gave Gary David's number on just the right day
when everything was
going wrong
or

seemingly.

*

PS:

Wasn't
it Rimbaud who said when the female
poets come, we won't even recognize them.
this was before pop stardom,
of course.

CRAZY

is an attempt to touch the untouchable & to release the power of the
untouchable. Some few references out of the ordinary: *Bharatya Natya
Sastra*, lst. Treatise on Indian poetry & music, *chod*, a Tibetan practice, of
offering, female lineage of Machig Labdron, well known to Burroughs &
Gysin who used its central tenant to define & refine the cut up technique
(see Days Lane by Terry Wilson).

Who am I,
a traveler, here, traveling through chakras
channels, inner body of heat, wisdom & desire &, of course,
to the geographic sites which formulate the refuge of the narrative.

Crazy goes beyond time, irrespective of formula. Please trace the
history of the Jews in Eastern Europe, 20th century, for further details
of the text. Namkhai Norbu is a contemporary master of Ati yoga—

Dzog Chen, the great perfection. A student once found a paper saying
that in prior incarnations he worked, as a master, to liberate beings
fr. Hell Realms—the student-translator covertly read the text.
When the master entered the hotel room

where the two were staying, the text had,
of course been put aside,
The master smiled & said,
go on reading.

War & famine mark
the millennium/ hopefully the
deep poetic is still accessible through sound,
both inner & outer, forgive me if I had no subject
to offer except the one I have offered. For
years I saw w. inner sight this book,
here it is, at last

**Crazy Louise or
La Conversazione Sacra**

& w. grateful thanks to poet & photographer Ira Cohen—1935-2011
who spent the last weeks of his life at 225 W. 106th Street NYC.
correcting this book in its last. printing of 25 copies.

*

On the day of our Lord
25.XII.2010
Crazy L.ouise
is dedicated to
RF
&
in memory of
Janine Pommy Vega
1942 – 2010

When mother love conflicts w. social facade, the dye is cast in favor of sympathy.
Blocked by appearance love comes through in the fierce play of imagination.

Allen Ginsberg

AMSTEL RIVER, MOKUM

Acknowledgments

The author extends her thanks: to the editors who published excerpts fr. this material; to the late Ira Cohen who diligently corrected it in the weeks of his decline & who, in his prime, shot the cover portrait; to Kelvin Daly, Lauren O'Connor & Virginia Tate for insightful council & inspired company in NYC; to Felix Offset, aka Felix Mansingh, in Amsterdam, for the original edition bound in 25 copies, followed by 15 unbound ones & to Bastiaan Lips, co-designer of the original; to Ed Goldberg for presenting it to the current publishers; & finally to Choegyal Namkhai Norbu, Ati Yoga Master; Dugu Choegyal Rinpoche, master painter of the Drukpa Kargyu; Dr.Trogawa Rinpoche, consummate medical practitioner; & Rabbi Rahamim Banin, who returned the spiritual teaching to the ghetto of Venice and gave me space to work on this & other manuscripts.

To Poets In Need & Gene Gawain for financial assistance; & to publishers George & Susan Quasha of Station Hill Press & Director Sam Truitt, for undertaking this project & for kindly considering the many details of its publication.

LLL
NYC 2014

About the Author

Louise Landes Levi is a poet/performer-translator/traveler and a founding member of Daniel Moore's Floating Lotus Magic Opera Company, America's first fusion orchestra. After receiving a BA, with Honors, from UC-Berkeley, and studying at Mills College with the sarangi-master Pandit Ram Narayan, she traveled alone overland to Afghanistan in the late 1960s and to India, via Istanbul, Tabriz, Mashed, Herat, Khandahar, Kabul, Peshawar, Rawalpundi and Lahore, to research North Indian *sangeet* (classical music) and its poetic tradition. Several translations followed: Rene Daumal's classic study of Indian Aesthetics, *RASA* (New Directions, 1982); from the Middle Hindi of Mira Bai, an archetypal singer-saint of the 16th century, *Sweet On My Lips: The Love Poems of Mira Bai* (Cool Grove Press, 1997, 2003 & 2016); and Henri Michaux's *Toward Totality: Selected Poems* (Shivastan, 2006). She has published more than a dozen books of poetry and autobiographical prose, including most recently: *Love Cantos, 1-5* (Jack In Your Box, 2011); *The Book L* (Cool Grove Press, 2010); *Tower 2/Tara or dc-x* (Il Bagatto, 2009); *Banana Baby*, with facing Italian translations by Alessandro Tuoni (Super Nova, 2006); and *Avenue A & Ninth Street* (Shivastan, 2004). Her electronic chapbooks may be found at the website Big Bridge. Her recordings include most recently: *From the Ming Oracle*, (Sloowax, 2014), an instrumental and spoken word compilation of her works from the late sixties to the near present; *City of Delirium* (Sloow Tapes, 2011); and the forthcoming LP *Colloidal Love Poem* (AudioMER.). John Giorno writes: 'Her poems sing in the mind and dance through the heart and throat, and arms & legs, w. great clarity and bliss. Louise is Saranswati, goddess of poetry." Levi has studied with such masters as Annapurna Devi, Ali Akbar Khan & La Monte Young. When not performing, she lives in a stone tower in Bagnore, Italy, with winter quarters in New York, her birthplace, and elsewhere.